© Copyright 2012 John F. Schmuecker

Table of Contents

What College Won't Teach You 1

What is a Credit Report? 3

Your Credit Score Affects Everything You Do in Life 7

Rule 1: Borrow to Establish Your Credit 11

Rule 2: Have Only One Credit Card 13

Rule 3: Pay It Off in Full Every Month 17

Rule 4: Borrow for Needs Not Wants 19

Rule 5: Don't Cosign for Friends 21

Rule 6: Get Your Personal Credit Report and Check Errors 23

Rule 7: Create a Budget and Stick to It 25

A final Note to Parents- The College Value Proposition 29

Appendix 1: Sample Credit Report and Credit Score 31

Appendix 2: Sample Budget for Your First Entry-Level Job 35

Appendix 3: Internet Sources for Credit Information 37

What College Won't Teach You

Most colleges and universities don't teach basic personal finance. Consequently, most kids enter the work force clueless about personal finance, credit card traps, and the disastrous consequences of a bad credit score or personal credit report on their lives.

If we can teach our high school seniors and freshmen in college how they get credit and how they can quickly ruin their own credit, we can better prepare them for the real world after graduation. If the recent economic crash taught us anything, it's that too much debt and poor credit ruined a lot of lives. I know finance. I've got an MBA, I've run companies, and I've just put two sons through four years of college. I've helped them navigate into their first jobs, and I've talked with hundreds of other kids about personal finances. All I need is twenty minutes of your time.

This could be the most important class you'll take in your life.

What is a Credit Report?

Personal Information

Registration Information
- **Name:** Stephen X. Smith
- **Address:** 123 Main Street, Anywhere, VA 12345
- **Social Security Number:** 022-22-2222

Identification Information

	Equifax	Experian	TransUnion
	Reported	Reported	Reported
Name:	JOHN Q PUBLIC	JOHN Q PUBLIC	JOHN Q PUBLIC
Social Security Number:	022-22-2222	022-22-2222	022-22-2222
Age or Date of Birth:	03/1958	03/1958	03/1958

Address Information

	Equifax	Experian	TransUnion
	Reported	Reported	Reported
Address:	123 MAIN ST ANYWHERE, VA 22222	123 MAIN ST ANYWHERE, VA 22222	123 MAIN ST ANYWHERE, VA 22222
Date Reported:	03/1999	01/2002	10/1999
	Reported	Reported	Reported
Address:	321 EXIT ST SOMEWHERE, VA 22222	321 EXIT ST SOMEWHERE, VA 22222	321 EXIT ST SOMEWHERE, VA 22222
Date Reported:	11/1998	12/2001	09/1999

Employment Information

	Equifax	Experian	TransUnion
	Reported	Reported	Not Reported
Employer:	ABC CORP	ABC CORP	
Address:			
Date Reported:	02/2001	02/2001	

Account Information

American Express

	Equifax	Experian	TransUnion
	Reported	Reported	Reported
Account Type:	REVOLVING	REVOLVING	REVOLVING
Account Number:	00726	00726	00726
Payment Responsibility:	Individual	Individual	Individual
Date Opened:	03/1991	03/1991	03/1991
Balance Date:	04/2002	04/2002	04/2002
Balance Amount:	$704	$704	$704
Monthly Payment:	$21	$21	$21
Credit Limit:	$704	$6416	$704
High Balance:			
Account Status:	AS AGREED	CURR ACCT	Paid as agreed
Past Due Amount:	$0	$0	$0
Comments:	Charge	Charge	Charge

EQUIFAX 3 in 1 Sample Credit Report

A credit report is built up from information collected by anyone who has given you credit. It includes how much you owe, and your repayment history. It includes money you owe on credit cards, car loans, student loans, utility company payments from cable TV, electric and gas companies, hospital bills, medical bills, rent payments on your apartment, mortgage payments, any public records like tax liens and bankruptcies, and many other sources. Information in this report will determine your credit score.

Let's take a look at how many things are influenced by your credit report:

1. Your chances of getting a job.

2. Your chances of renting an apartment or getting a mortgage later in life.

3. Your chances of getting a car loan.

4. Your chances of getting insurance for your car.

5. Your chances of getting married.

Let's look quickly at all of the five things above.

Your Job – Every job applicant fills out a job application that asks a lot of questions. Included is your agreement to allow the employer to do a complete background check on you, including a full credit check. Employers get very nervous when they see applicants with poor credit scores. How responsible will they be if they can't even manage their own money? How honest will they be if they are deeply in debt, have defaulted on loans, or have been turned over for collection? Why choose an applicant with a poor credit report and score when there are many others with good credit?

Your New Apartment – Again, most landlords require a full application that allows a full credit check on you. It is very difficult for a landlord to remove a tenant who does not pay on time. If your credit score is low and credit report is bad, you will not be allowed to rent.

Your Car Loan – If you really want that super low interest rate car loan, read the small print. You need a top credit score to qualify. OK, some used car dealers say they will finance bad credit accounts. But do you really want to pay 25% interest on a car loan?

Your Car Insurance – On your application for car insurance, you authorize a full credit check. Insurance companies have long known the correlation of bad credit to claims filed. They also have to make sure they get paid.

Poor credit can drive up your insurance rates or put you into a higher risk pool.

Your Chances Of Getting Married And Staying Married – There is a limit to what love can conquer. Many couples that plan to get married now have a frank discussion on how they stand financially. If you have poor credit and a huge amount of debt, especially student debt, who wants to take on that additional burden in marriage? A recent news story in the New York Times reported more couples breaking up before marriage over financial issues, including large student loan balances.

Despite four years of higher education and a college degree, most people are clueless about the total meaning of personal credit and their credit score. By the time they realize their mistake, it's too late.

You can see a sample credit report for a recently graduated college student in Appendix 1.

Your Credit Score Affects Everything You Do in Life

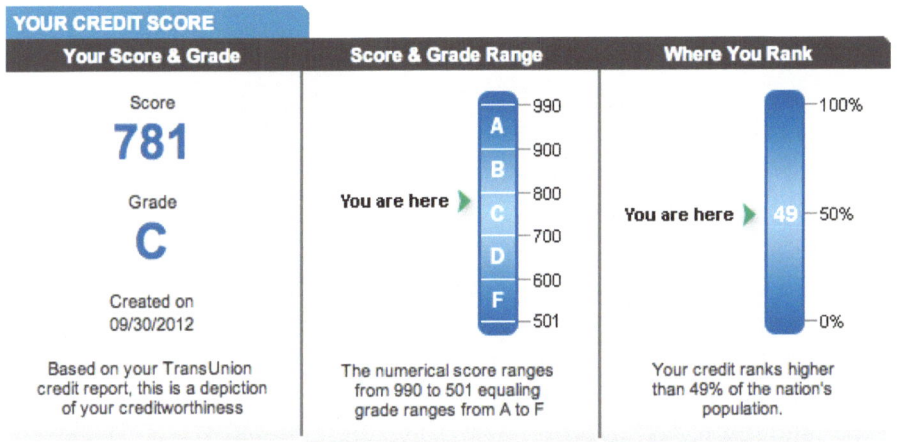

One simple three-digit number can ruin your life or can make it easy. It's your credit score and it sums up your credit report.

The New VantageScore®

The three credit reporting companies – Equifax®, Experian®, and TransUnion®, recently created the VantageScore®. Scores range from a low of 501 to a high of 990. You are rated on an easy to understand grading system (like school) as follows:

A: 900-990 - Very Good or Super Prime credit category

B: 800 to 899 - Good or Prime Plus credit category

C: 700-799 - Fair or Prime credit category

D: 600-699 – Poor or Non Prime credit category

F: 501-599 - Very Poor or High Risk credit category

While there are many variations in terms of factors and percentages used by all three credit reporting agencies that determine your credit score, the following is a good way to understand the factors.

Your credit score is generally determined by the following information:

1. **28% of your score comes from your bill payment history.** If you are late on payments or skip payments, your credit score will go down.

2. **23% of your score is determined by your credit utilization.** This means how much credit you have been given by lenders such as credit card companies, car loans, and student loans, versus how much you have used. A simple example is a credit card company that gives you a $2,000 credit limit. If you have used $1,800, that is a high utilization, and that can lower your score.

3. **9% of your score comes from your credit history.** How long have you had that credit card? How long have you had your car loan? What is the credit mix? The longer you have had credit and paid on time, the better the score. Getting a credit card in college, paying on time and paying it off every month will improve your score. Borrowing up to the credit limit and keeping high balances and paying the monthly minimum will lower your score.

4. **9% of your score comes from the types of credit you have.** You have revolving loans like bank credit cards and department store charge cards; term loans like car loans that have a fixed repayment schedule such as 48 months; and mortgages. A high use of credit cards with large balances will hurt your credit score.

5. **30% of your score comes from recent credit.** Lenders get nervous when people apply for lots of credit and open new credit accounts in a short period of time. They usually monitor your credit report to look at your payment history with other lenders and to check for excessive debt loads.

6. **1% of your score comes from how much credit you have available.**

Of these six components, **paying your bill on time every month, and keeping your debt very low compared to your available credit, are the two biggest factors.** That means for college students, pay off your credit cards every month, pay your cable and utility bills on time and keep your outstanding debt low, especially student loans.

Note on the FICO® credit score

Although all three credit reporting agencies created the VantageScore® in 2012, some lenders and Equifax may use the FICO® score. It is similar to the VantageScore®. It is a rating between 350 (the lowest) and 850 (the highest).

Generally, FICO credit scores are rated as follows:

- Excellent -750 to 850

- Good - 660 to 749

- Fair - 620 to 659

- Poor - 350 to 619

You can achieve an excellent credit score by following the seven simple rules that follow.

Rule 1: Borrow to Establish Your Credit

At some point in your life, you're going to need credit. $20,000 cars, and $150,000 houses are normally too expensive to pay in cash. You will need to borrow money to pay these bills.

Back before the economic crash of 2009, it seems like anyone could get credit. Everyone over 18, including college students, were flooded with credit card offers, low-interest car loans and no-income verification mortgages. I was amazed one day when my son, who worked a part time job in high school, got a Visa credit card from the Old Navy Store with a $500 credit limit (and an 19% interest rate). When I asked him how he got it, he said he signed up at the store to get an extra 20% off a shirt he bought. Times have changed but lenders still need to lend and borrowers still need to borrow.

How do you establish a credit history?

Get a Credit Card: The most common way students establish credit is by having a parent cosign – or guarantee – the repayment of a credit card in your name. All major credit cards offer this type of card, including Visa, MasterCard, Discover and American Express. The credit card limit (how much you can charge) is typically what the parents have on their card. Carefully used and repaid every month on time, you can establish your own credit since the credit history is reported for the student. Older working students can often get a low limit credit card on their own without a cosigner because they have a job and an income. As charges are repaid on time, your credit limit slowly increases. Larger purchases that you charge and pay off immediately can increase your credit limit.

An option to a regular credit card is getting a secured credit card. This is not a debit card that subtracts money out of an existing bank account like a checking or savings account. In this case, you deposit the money up front, typically $300 to $500, and charge against it. Over time, you can get this secure credit card converted to a standard credit card if the card is managed properly. You do not want to get the "over-limit" option if it is offered because there is a big fee every time you go over your deposited amount.

Get a Car Loan: A car is often the first major purchase a student will make. The parents can cosign the loan and the credit is reported, under the student's name, to the credit agency. This is what's called a term loan – you pay off the borrowed amount over a fixed term of months such as 36 months.

Get a Checking Account: Parents can open a checking account for their kids and link it to their own bank account. This allows them to monitor the student's spending and set up automatic payments for credit cards or loans to prevent big late-payments fees. Most banks offer "no fee or low fee" student checking accounts. Automatic payments can also prevent missed payment fees that will lower your credit rating or increase your interest rate.

With a carefully monitored credit card, car loan or student checking account, you can teach your kids the basics of budgeting and personal finance and establish a credit history. All major banks have excellent websites featuring smart tips on personal budgeting and finance.

Rule 2: Have Only One Credit Card

Everybody is going to push a credit card at you. Banks, gasoline companies, airlines, retail merchants like Amazon, Sears, JC Penney, Gap, Macy's, and maybe your university. Some colleges have a relationship with a bank and invite the preferred bank to campus to push their credit cards on students. According to Credit.com, over 50% of recent college graduates had four credit cards. Don't be one of them.

Only have one credit card.

One major bank credit card (Visa or MasterCard) which is accepted everywhere, is all you need to make credit purchases. It will provide you with a reasonable credit limit based on your age and financial situation. A separate Gap, Old Navy or other in-store merchant card may earn you 20% off a one-time purchase, but increases the temptation to borrow more and to pay only the minimum due each month. It's easy to congratulate yourself for only borrowing $300 on your Abercrombie & Fitch card, while conveniently ignoring that you've got another $500 on your Ikea card, and another $200 on that Staples card. Store credit cards commonly charge higher interest rates than a standard bank credit card. Finally, multiple monthly credit card payments are also harder to manage. There are more bills to misplace, more chances to forget a monthly payment, or pay one late.

What is the best credit card to get? Here's what to look for:

1. No Annual Fee - Skip the Gold and Platinum cards with their $75 annual fee. Get a card with no annual fee.

2. Lowest annual percentage rate - ("APR") The lowest rate offered is zero -- if you pay it off each month. However, if you must run a balance for emergencies be prepared to pay hefty rates of 16% to 20% or more. Even people with the best credit ratings often pay 13-15%. Look for the lowest rate, and beware of low introductory rates which jump significantly after a few months.

3. Late fees - Almost all credit cards automatically charge a late fee of, on average, $35. If you owe $300, that's almost 12% of what you owe. You are generally given 21 days from the statement date to pay in full to avoid an interest charge.

4. Maximum Penalty Rate - If you miss one payment or are late even once, most credit cards can and do increase your interest rate to the penalty rate. On most credit cards, this is 29.99%.

5. Cash Advance Rate - You never want to use this. This is usually between 5-10% higher than the already high standard rates of 16-20%.

6. Over Credit Limit Fees - This is also very high and varies widely but it is similar to the late payment fee. You can and should opt out of this feature if you are offered.

Warning!

Multiple, major, well-known credit card issuers in the last two years have been caught and fined by the U.S. Consumer Financial Protection Bureau for using pressure or even outright deception to try and get consumers to buy costly add-on services to their credit cards – credit monitoring, payment protection, identity theft protection, etc. For most people, these expensive, extra services are unnecessary. Some card companies will even enroll you in programs without your consent. So make sure you read the fine print in your contract, monitor your bill closely every month, and immediately challenge any charge you don't recognize or understand. Note, your maximum liability if your credit card is lost or stolen is generally $50 under the Fair Credit Billing Act.

Rule 3: Pay It Off in Full Every Month

The temptation to overspend on credit cards is great and the minimum payments are very small, so the average student graduates with $4,100 in credit card debt. Typical interest rates are 18% on most credit cards. If you miss payments or have bad credit the rate is typically 29.99%. Late payments or missed payments, over limit penalties, drive down your credit score. Also, too much credit card debt in relation to your total credit hurts your score.

In a simple example, If you owe $1,000 on your card at 18% interest you are paying $180 in interest per year. Pay late and it will cost you another $35 fee and will escalate your rate to 29.99%. Your annual interest cost just increased to $300! You now are paying $335 per year on a $1,000 credit card debt.

Rule 4: Borrow For "Needs" Not "Wants"

In life there are "needs" and there are "wants." It is better to learn this now rather than later in life. Needs are dorm food, a dorm room; a ten year old Honda, a break from classes, a phone and a computer.

Wants are Starbucks coffee, off-campus apartment with flat panel TV and cable, a BMW, Spring break vacation, the newest iPhone, a $1000 laptop, and iPad.

If you can pay for wants without borrowing, go right ahead. But if you have to borrow the money and pay the credit card company 18% interest, do without until you have saved enough to buy it with cash.

Failure to live within your means is the primary cause of bad credit.

Rule 5: Don't Cosign for Friends

Never cosign on a credit card, utility account like cable, electric or gas, or student loan for someone else, including friends or people you are in a relationship with. If you have good credit and cosign for someone who does not, you are totally responsible for that loan or bill until it's paid off. Sure you believe you will be together forever and the loan will be paid every month and on time, but college romances and dorm friendships are notoriously fragile. If they default, it hurts your credit and you may have to repay the debt of someone else. **Accounts turned over for collection or written off by the lender stay on your credit report for seven years or longer and will severely reduce your credit score.**

My son had a friend, a senior in college who was working many jobs and had good credit. His girlfriend, who had over $75,000 in student loans asked him to cosign a $5,000 student loan "for a short time until her debt was refinanced" since she was at her credit limit. They broke up one year later. The loan was never refinanced and the loan went to collection two years later when she defaulted. As cosigner, he was liable for the total debt that had grown to over $8,000 including late fees and penalties. His credit rating was lowered by 100 points when it was reported on his credit. To add insult to injury, he was forced to pay off her student loan in full to get his credit partially restored. Never cosign a loan unless you are prepared to repay it.

My other son had a college friend who cosigned on a cable television account that was used in a shared apartment off campus. When they moved out and the semester ended, the final bill was never paid and went to collection. Even though he was not the primary account holder and did not get the bills, he cosigned. The collection account was reported on his credit report and reduced his credit score. He had to pay the last bill, plus collection, and it will remain on his credit report for seven years.

Rule 6: Get Your Personal Credit Report and Check for Errors

Get Your Free Credit Report Annually

There are three main companies that issue credit reports and scores – Equifax,® TransUnion® and Experian®. All three contain information about your credit history with minor differences. **By law, you are entitled to get a free copy of each one every 12 months.** Despite all the Internet ads, **there is only one free national website to get your free report. It is found at www.annualcreditreport.com.** You can order online or call 1-877-322-8228, or complete the Annual Credit Report Request Form and mail it to: Annual Credit Report Request Service, P.O. Box 105281, Atlanta, GA 30348-5281. You can print it from ftc.gov/credit. Do not contact the three nationwide consumer reporting companies individually. They provide free annual credit reports only through www. annualcreditreport. com

Check Your Credit Report For Errors

Given the volume of transactions posted by credit report companies, errors are not uncommon. You need to get a copy each year of your credit report and check it for errors. You have the right to dispute and have corrections made to your report. Information is included on how to do this when you get your free report. Don't wait until you apply for a car loan or an apartment lease to find out an error needs to be fixed. It may take months to correct.

You Have To Pay For Your Credit Score

Unfortunately, you have to pay to get your credit score. When you get your free credit report from Equifax®, TransUnion® or Experian®, you will be offered the option of buying your credit score. You need to do this. It is usually under $10 to get your score. Your score can vary slightly between the three companies but should be very similar. Note: do not take the free credit score offered by all three companies. You will be directed to sign up for expensive annual monitoring that you do not need in order to get a free score.

Do You Need A Credit Score
From All Three Credit Reporting Companies?

Generally all three reports and credit scores are going to be very similar. You will only need to pay for one credit score since all three scores are usually very similar. However, you should get a copy of all three free credit reports during the year to check for errors or problems in reporting.

Rule 7: Create A Budget And Stick To It

According to the Federal Reserve survey of consumer finances, almost half of Americans spend more than they make. Since the average college student leaves college with $25,000 of student loans and over $4,000 of credit card debt, you need a serious budget in place before you graduate.

Appendix 2 has a typical monthly budget for a new graduate earning $35,000 a year showing repayments of $25,000 in student loans and $4,000 of credit card debt, the national averages. It goes without saying that your son or daughter will most likely be sharing an apartment with one or two other friends found on Craigslist given their debts and starting salary. They will also be broke each month.

What happens if you default on a student loan?

1. The government can garnish (seize or withhold) up to 15% of your wages.

2. The government can take your federal and state income tax refunds.

3. You may be charged late fees of up to 6% of each late payment.

4. Collection charges of up to 25% may also be deducted from each payment on your defaulted loans, slowing the repayment and increasing your costs.

5. The government can block the renewal of professional licenses.

6. The default may prevent you from getting credit cards, auto loans and home mortgages and may make it harder to rent an apartment or get a job. You will be ineligible for more federal student aid. You may be harassed by collectors.

> ***NOTE-* You cannot get rid of your college loans by filing bankruptcy.**

The time to teach students about personal financing and budgeting is during college, not after. You should talk to them and work out a careful budget of income and expense. Hopefully they will not make any bad mistakes before they graduate that can hurt their future credit.

The key is to draw up the budget together and stick to it. The second step is to monitor it every month.

If you are smart and set up joint accounts with your child and link their checking account and credit card to your accounts, you can help them monitor their expenses each month and update the budget.

One of the best gifts you can give to your kids is to set up a monthly budget with them when they graduate and get their first job. Gross pay and net pay are two very different things and need to be discussed. If they built up their credit score and have learned to live within their means, they will enjoy great financial success. There is no better gift you can give them than to teach them how to be financially secure in life.

There are three great maxims for being financially secure in life.

1. Always spend less than you make.

2. Know the difference between a need and a want.

3. The most difficult thing in life is being content with what you have.

A Final Note For Parents - The College Value Proposition

It is your decision as to what college your son or daughter can attend if you are paying the bills. If you or your child are taking out loans for college, consider the value proposition of a low cost two year community college with a transfer to a state four year university versus a high cost private university. According to the National Center for Educational Statistics, the average cost for tuition room and board at a private not for profit college is $36,300. For a public state college it is $13,600. Is the private college worth the value proposition of the extra $22,700 of debt per year?

There are a lot of students who graduated from expensive private universities with liberal arts degrees and big student loans, who are waiting on tables or "trying to figure out" what they want to do several years after graduation. Generally, they have no better chance of getting a job than the graduate from the state university.

Second, if your high school senior has no idea what he wants as his college major, they can attend a low cost community college until they sort it out. Colleges are in the business of making money and switching majors late can cost you another semester or full year of college. Are you prepared to pay another $10,000 to $40,000 while they sort this out? Consider the following facts from the College Board :

1. Tuition and fees at community colleges average only 36.2% of the average four year public college tuition and fees. Some community colleges charge as little as $2,000 per year.

2. Community Colleges are the largest post secondary education segment.

3. The majority of community college students plan to transfer to four year colleges.

4. Four year colleges are making it much easier to transfer from community colleges. In fact many four year colleges automatically accept graduates from many community colleges.

If your son or daughter graduates with $25,000 in debt and makes $35,000 a year, they will be broke every month or living with you. Do you want them to move back home because they can't afford to rent? Do you plan to help them repay their student loan debt so they don't default? Are you planning on helping them financially each month because their credit is ruined and they can't earn enough to live on?

In summary, the best value proposition is the lowest cost four-year in state college education and graduating with the lowest possible student loan debt. For students who have no clue as to what their major will be or what they want to do in life, start off with the two-year community college. They can always transfer to a four-year state college when they figure it out.

Appendix 1:
Sample Credit Report and Credit Score

File Number:
365927916

You may see that TransUnion has enriched your credit report with additional personal and financial information not previously retained in our production database. This data can enable you and your creditors to see a more complete picture of how you have managed your credit over time.

-Begin Credit Report-

Personal Information

You have been on our files since 12/18/2007

SSN:
012-34-5677
Date of Birth:
04/22/1988

Names Reported:
EVAN J. ESTRADA

Addresses Reported:
Address
42 MAIN ST, HARTFORD, CT 06834

Date Reported
02/25/2012

Telephone Numbers Reported:
516-221-1681

Account Information

Typically, creditors report any changes made to your account information monthly. This means that some accounts listed below may not reflect the most recent activity until the creditor's next reporting. This information may include things such as balances, payments, dates, remarks, ratings, etc. The key(s) below are provided to help you understand some of the account information that could be reported.

Rating Key
Some creditors report the timeliness of your payments each month in relation to your agreement with them. The ratings in the key below describe the payments that may be reported by your creditors. Any rating that is shaded indicates that it is considered adverse. Please note: Some but not all of these ratings may be present in your credit report.

N/R	X	OK	30	60	90	120	COL	VS	RPO	C/O	FC
Not Reported	Unknown	Current	30 days late	60 days late	90 days late	120 + days late	Collection	Voluntary Surrender	Repo-ssession	Charge Off	Foreclosure

Satisfactory Accounts

For your protection, your account numbers have been partially masked, and in some cases scrambled.

WELLS FARGO CARD SERVICE #123456789101****
CREDIT BUREAU DISPUTE RES
P O BOX 14517
DES MOINES, IA 50306
(800) 642-4720

Date Opened:
03/31/2009
Responsibility:
Joint Account
Account Type:
Revolving Account
Loan Type:CREDIT CARD

Balance:
$0
Date Updated:
09/25/2012
Last Payment Made:
09/18/2012
High Balance:
$1,502
Credit Limit:
$2,400

Pay Status:
Current; Paid or Paying as Agreed
Date Paid:
09/18/2012

Rating	08/2012	07/2012	06/2012	05/2012	04/2012	03/2012	02/2012	01/2012	12/2011	11/2011
	OK	OK	OK	OK	OK	OK	OK	OK	OK	OK

Rating	10/2011	09/2011	08/2011	07/2011	06/2011	05/2011	04/2011	03/2011	02/2011	01/2011
	OK	OK	OK	OK	OK	OK	OK	OK	OK	OK

Rating	12/2010	11/2010	10/2010	09/2010	08/2010	07/2010	06/2010	05/2010	04/2010	03/2010
	OK	OK	OK	OK	OK	OK	OK	OK	OK	OK

Rating	02/2010	01/2010	12/2009	11/2009	10/2009	09/2009	08/2009	07/2009	06/2009	05/2009
	OK	OK	OK	OK	OK	OK	OK	OK	OK	OK

Rating	04/2009	03/2009
	OK	OK

WELLS FARGO CARD SERVICE #101987654321****
CREDIT BUREAU RESOLUTION
P O BOX 14517
DES MOINES, IA 50306
(800) 642-4720

Date Opened:
05/18/2012
Responsibility:
Individual Account
Account Type:
Revolving Account
Loan Type:CREDIT CARD

Balance:
$1,908
Date Updated:
09/25/2012
Last Payment Made:
09/18/2012
High Balance:
$3,197
Credit Limit:
$7,500

Pay Status:
Current; Paid or Paying as Agreed
Terms:
$45 per month

Rating	08/2012	07/2012	06/2012	05/2012
	OK	OK	OK	OK

Regular Inquiries

Regular Inquiries are posted when someone accesses your credit information from TransUnion. The presence of an inquiry means that the company listed received your credit information on the dates specified. These inquiries will remain on your credit file for up to 2 years.

AVALON RIVERVIEW via SAFERENT

7300 WESTMORE RD S
ROCKVILLE, MD 20850
(800) 999-0350

Requested On:
08/29/2012
InquiryType:
Individual
Permissible Purpose:
ACCOUNT REVIEW

Promotional Inquiries

The companies listed below received your name, address and other limited information about you so they could make a firm offer of credit or insurance. They did not receive your full credit report. These inquiries are not seen by anyone but you and do not affect your score.

DISCOVER FINCL SVC LLC

PO BOX 15316
WILMINGTON, DE 19850-5316
Phone number not available

Requested On:
09/06/2012, 08/30/2012, 08/09/2012, 08/02/2012, 07/26/2012

GEICO

1 GEICO PLZ
WASHINGTON, DC 20076-0003
Phone number not available

Requested On:
08/30/2012

AMERICAN EXPRESS

PO BOX 981537
EL PASO, TX 79998
(800) 874-2717

Requested On:
08/11/2012, 05/13/2012, 04/07/2012, 03/10/2012, 09/11/2011

CAPITAL ONE BANK USA NA

PO BOX 30281
SALT LAKE CITY, UT 84130
(800) 258-9319

Requested On:
06/26/2012, 05/29/2012, 10/23/2011, 09/27/2011

THE TRAVELERS COMPANIES

1 TOWER SQ
18CP
HARTFORD, CT 06183-0001
(866) 240-2682

Requested On:
01/05/2012

FIRST USA

800 BROOKSEDGE BLVD
WESTERVILLE, OH 43081-2822
Phone number not available

Requested On:
10/31/2011, 10/03/2011

Additional Information

The following disclosure of information is provided as a courtesy to you. This information is not part of your TransUnion credit report, but may be provided when TransUnion receives an inquiry about you from an authorized party. This additional information can include Special Messages, Possible Office of Foreign Assets Control ("OFAC") Name Matches, Income Verification and Inquiry Analysis information. Any of the previously listed information that pertains to you will be listed below.

Inquiry Analysis

The companies that request your credit report must first provide certain information about you. Within the past 90 days, companies that requested your report provided the following information.

AVALON RIVERVIEW via SAFERENT

Requested On:
08/29/2012
Identifying information they provided:
ERAN ESTRADA
42 MAIN STREET
HARTFORD, CT 06834

-End of Additional Information-

| AnnualCreditReport.com | ▶ Return to AnnualCreditReport.com | ▶ Frequently Asked Questions |

 Trans**Union**.

Your Credit Score

| Credit Report | **Score** |

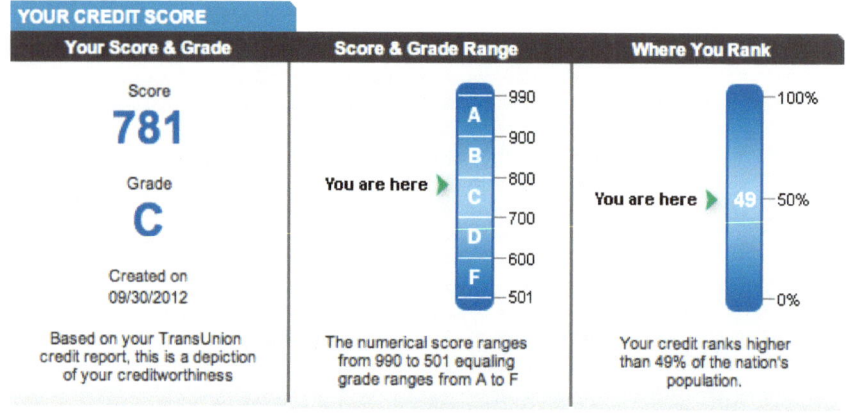

About your TransUnion Personal Credit Score
Your TransUnion Personal Credit Score is displayed above, and was calculated with the VantageScore credit scoring formula. Your credit score is a snapshot of the contents of your credit report at the time the score was calculated. Using objective, impartial formulas to translate the contents of your credit report into a 3-digit score enables lenders to evaluate your application for credit in a fast, fair and more objective manner. Remember, we constantly update the information contained in your credit report, so your TransUnion Personal Credit Score only represents the score a lender would receive if they requested it today.

Summary
Given that you have an average credit score, it may be difficult for you to qualify for the best credit offers. Prepare yourself to pay higher fees and interest rates, as well as make deposits and down payments. If you are applying for a credit card, be prepared for the possibility of lower or no lines of credit and high interest rates. To increase your borrowing power and credit score, prove that you are creditworthy by always paying your bills on time. Your credit score can see dramatic improvements over time.

Factors that impact your score:

1. You have too few credit accounts.

A healthy balance of credit and loan accounts is key to achieving a high credit score. It is important to build a record of responsible credit use over time with different types of accounts.

2. Time since oldest account opened is too recent.

Time is an important factor for a healthy credit score. Giving the accounts time to mature may allow creditors to better understand how you pay your debts.

3. You have no retail revolving accounts that can be used in determining a credit score.

A healthy balance of credit and loan accounts is key to achieving a high credit score. It is important to build a record of responsible credit use over time with different types of accounts.

4. You have no real estate accounts that can be used in determining a credit score.

A healthy balance of credit and loan accounts is key to achieving a high credit score. It is important to build a record of responsible credit use over time with different types of accounts.

Note: In addition to the factors listed above, the number of Inquiries on your credit report has adversely affected your credit score.

Answers About Credit Scores

· How are credit scores used?

A credit score is just one of several factors a company usually uses when deciding to extend credit, give insurance coverage or provide financial services to you. A variety of other factors will be considered, such as length of employment, income or previous experience with you. Depending on what you are applying for, different companies weigh each of these factors differently. By using a credit score, they can evaluate your application quickly, fairly and consistently.

· How can I improve my credit score?

A credit score is a snapshot of the contents of your credit report at the time it was calculated. Long-term, responsible credit behavior is the most effective way to improve future scores. Pay bills on time, lower balances and use credit wisely to improve your score over time. You should also review your credit report to ensure it is accurate.

· How do inquiries affect my credit score?

When your credit is checked by a business for the purpose of an application a "hard inquiry" appears on your credit report. These inquiries can affect your credit score; and typically they have only a small impact. Delinquencies, balances owed, and the length of time you have used credit are all more important. Inquiries have a greater impact if you have a limited credit history.

Additional Information

The TransUnion Personal Credit Score is provided to help you better understand how lenders view your credit report. It is not an endorsement or a determination of your qualification for a loan. The VantageScore credit scoring model was used for this Score Analysis and is not necessarily the same scoring model that may be used by a lender. The resulting credit score may not be identical in every respect to any consumer credit score produced by any other company. Any credit information that has not yet been reported to TransUnion will not be reflected in your consumer disclosure or score. Also, some items disputed directly with creditors are not incorporated in the assessment of your credit score.

Appendix 2:
Sample Budget For Your New Job

Income $35,000 per year before taxes
$25,000 student loan balance, $4,000 credit card debt

Personal Monthly Budget

PROJECTED MONTHLY INCOME		
Income 1		$2,916
Extra income		$0
Total monthly income		**$2,916**

ACTUAL MONTHLY INCOME		
Income 1		$2,916
Extra income		$0
Total monthly income		**$2,916**

PROJECTED BALANCE (Projected income minus expenses)	$58
ACTUAL BALANCE (Actual income minus expenses)	$58
DIFFERENCE (Actual minus projected)	$0

HOUSING	Projected Cost	Actual Cost	Difference
Mortgage or rent	$800	$800	$0
Phone	$50	$50	$0
Electricity	$35	$35	$0
Gas	$50	$50	$0
Water and sewer	$0	$0	$0
Cable	$50	$50	$0
Waste removal	$0	$0	$0
Maintenance or repairs	$0	$0	$0
Supplies	$0	$0	$0
Other	$0	$0	$0
Subtotals	$985	$985	$0

TRANSPORTATION	Projected Cost	Actual Cost	Difference
Vehicle payment			$0
Bus/taxi fare			$0
Insurance	$100	$100	$0
Licensing			$0
Fuel	$100	$100	$0
Maintenance	$50	$50	$0
Other			$0
Subtotals	$250	$250	$0

INSURANCE	Projected Cost	Actual Cost	Difference
Home			$0
Health	$75	$75	$0
Life			$0
Other			$0
Subtotals	$75	$75	$0

FOOD	Projected Cost	Actual Cost	Difference
Groceries	$200	$200	$0
Dining out	$50	$50	$0
Other	$50	$50	$0
Subtotals	$300	$300	$0

PETS	Projected Cost	Actual Cost	Difference
Food			$0
Medical			$0
Grooming			$0
Toys			$0
Other			$0
Subtotals	$0	$0	$0

PERSONAL CARE	Projected Cost	Actual Cost	Difference
Medical			$0
Hair/nails	$20	$20	$0
Clothing	$20	$20	$0
Dry cleaning			$0
Health club	$25	$25	$0
Organization dues or fees			$0
Other			$0
Subtotals	$65	$65	$0

ENTERTAINMENT	Projected Cost	Actual Cost	Difference
Video/DVD			$0
CDs			$0
Movies			$0
Concerts			$0
Sporting events			$0
Live theater			$0
Other			$0
Other			$0
Other			$0
Subtotals			

LOANS	Projected Cost	Actual Cost	Difference
Personal			$0
Student	$288	$288	$0
Credit card	$150	$150	$0
Credit card			$0
Credit card			$0
Other			$0
Subtotals	$438	$438	$0

TAXES	Projected Cost	Actual Cost	Difference
Federal	$480	$480	
State	$175	$175	
Local			$0
Other			$0
Subtotals	$655	$655	

SAVINGS OR INVESTMENTS	Projected Cost	Actual Cost	Difference
Retirement account	$90	$90	$0
Investment account			$0
Other			$0
Subtotals	$90	$90	$0

GIFTS AND DONATIONS	Projected Cost	Actual Cost	Difference
Charity 1			$0
Charity 2			$0
Charity 3			$0
Subtotals	$0	$0	$0

LEGAL	Projected Cost	Actual Cost	Difference
Attorney			$0
Alimony			$0
Payments on lien or judgment			$0
Other			$0
Subtotals	$0	$0	$0

TOTAL PROJECTED COST	$2,858
TOTAL ACTUAL COST	$2,858
TOTAL DIFFERENCE	$0

Appendix 3:
Great Sources of Credit Information

www.credit.com - great source for personal credit information.

www.bankrate.com - great source for credit card and loan information, loan calculators

www.credit.com - how credit scores are calculated, general credit information.

Great Sources for College Cost Information

www.finaid.org - financial aid information

www.collegeboard.org - general information on college costs and options

www.ingramcontent.com/pod-product-compliance
Lightning Source LLC
Chambersburg PA
CBHW041114180526
45172CB00001B/244